Charlotte the Shark Won't Go to Sleep

By Catherine Tally
Illustrated by Ani Maqoyan

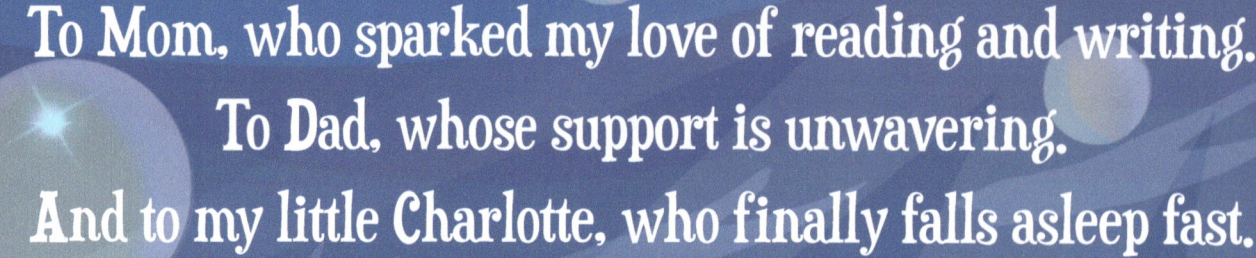

To Mom, who sparked my love of reading and writing.
To Dad, whose support is unwavering.
And to my little Charlotte, who finally falls asleep fast.

Charlotte the Shark Won't Go to Sleep
Copyright 2023 by Catherine Tally | instagram.com/tally_cat_02_
Illustrated by Ani Maqoyan | behance.net/d9c2501e
All rights reserved. No portion of this book may be reproduced, stored in a retrieval system, or transmitted in any form or by any means—electronic, mechanical, photocopy, recording, scanning, or other—except for brief quotations for review or citing purposes, without the prior written permission of the author.
Published by Argyle Fox Publishing | argylefoxpublishing.com
ISBN 978-1-953259-61-5

She laughed,
   swam,
      and played
         with friends
            every day.

But at bedtime each night, she shouted, "NO WAY!"

"Not tired! Need to potty! Want my sippy cup!"
The excuses poured out of the little shark pup*.

*Baby shark

Charlotte snuggled with Mommy,
as hours ticked by.
She needed to sleep,
but refused to try!

"Please sleep," Mommy begged.
"We're all tired now.
Your bed's nice and warm.
Here's your little sea cow*."

*Manatee

"Too dark!" Charlotte yelled, and dove into a fit.
"But Charlotte," Mommy sighed, "your night-light is lit."

Her stack of books had been finished, every one read.

But she still begged for more. "One more story!" she said.

By the moonlight's glow, Mommy read another book, as Charlotte's eyes grew heavy with that sleepy look.

Finally, it happened,
after the end had been read—
at long last, Charlotte
was asleep in her bed.

Mommy stroked Charlotte's head
with a tender, gentle fin.
It was just past twelve,
but this still seemed a win.

Some sharks are full of energy, always wand'ring about.

keep a smile and be patient.
These stormy seas won't last.

One day even sharks like Charlotte . . .

. . . will fall asleep fast.

CPSIA information can be obtained
at www.ICGtesting.com
Printed in the USA
JSHW071133090623
42921JS00004B/157